# Panda Kindergarten

### By Joanne Ryder
### Photographs by Dr. Katherine Feng

SOUTH SHORE BRANCH
2505 E. 73rd STREET
CHICAGO, ILLINOIS 60649

### Collins
*An Imprint of HarperCollins Publishers*

R0423022619
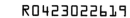

One panda cub is a sight to see.
Two panda cubs together is rare.
But imagine seeing
sixteen young giant pandas all at once!
Meet a panda kindergarten class
at the Wolong Nature Reserve in China,
where pandas are protected,
loved, and given great care.

Each cub is born

in a cozy room,

on a soft bed of straw.

A newborn cub is fuzzy and pink.

After a few weeks it starts to look

like its black-and-white mother.

An ever-so-big mother panda
carries her ever-so-tiny baby,
holding it firmly but tenderly.
She guides her new cub,
which cannot see her,
to rest on her broad, furry chest
and drink her fresh milk.

All the young cubs
are watched over by their mothers
and by kind, trained people.
Pandas often have twins,
but a mother
can care for only one cub at a time.

The other twin
needs to be fed
and kept healthy
and protected
in a nearby panda nursery.

As the small bears grow,

the skilled and helpful people

and the mother panda swap cubs

so each twin gets constant care,

and both share time with their mother.

With such a loving team,

each panda cub grows and grows.

Slowly its eyes open wide,

and it begins to see its mother's furry face

and other faces full of smiles.

When the panda cubs
are big enough to leave
their nursery and their mothers,
they are ready to have new adventures
and to make new friends
in panda kindergarten.
Here come the kindergartners!
Look at them go!

The young pandas
have their own
panda playground,
full of places
where cubs can
swing and climb
and play
with their new friends.
Pandas that play together
may learn to be
comfortable with each other
as cubs and as adults.

In their outdoor playground
the curious cubs
learn exciting things
about their world.
They discover
snow is cold
and very slippery.

Pandas always
find new ways to play,
like tugging and tearing,
and touching their toes.
To a panda cub,
almost anything
can be a toy.

Bolder and stronger,
cubs try new things,
climbing high and dangling
until . . .
it's time for lunch
in the panda kindergarten.

With so much to do
and so much to discover,
lively little bears
start feeling tired and sleepy.
It's time for cubs
to take a nap.

The young pandas
will be together
in panda kindergarten
for about a year.
As they grow older,
some will stay
in their safe Wolong home
and have cubs of their own.

One day
some may be chosen
to leave and live
in the bamboo forests
in the tall, misty mountains nearby.
Then the rare pandas
born in Wolong
would roam free and wild,
able to use the skills they
learned when they were small.

Learning from each other
and from the people who care for them,
the pandas born in Wolong
are on a special journey
that gives hope to pandas everywhere
and to all who love them.

# FAST FACTS
## ABOUT GIANT PANDAS

- A newborn giant panda is the size of a stick of butter and weighs about four ounces.

- Giant pandas are black-and-white bears. Like other bears, they are good climbers.

- An adult panda can weigh well over 200 pounds.

- Pandas make many sounds, including barks, honks, and growls. Very young cubs squeal loudly.

- In the wild, giant pandas mainly eat bamboo. They can eat 40 pounds of bamboo leaves each day!

- Low birthrates, food shortages, and poachers threaten the survival of pandas.

- As endangered animals, only about 1600 wild giant pandas live in the bamboo forests of southwest China.

- The giant panda is an unofficial national mascot of China.

To Jackson, Sam, and Matthew Yep, with love —J.R.

To the researchers and staff of the China Conservation and Research Center for the Giant Panda for their cooperation and enduring patience, without which the photos in this book would not be possible.
—K.F.

SOUTH SHORE BRANCH
2505 E. 73rd STREET
CHICAGO, ILLINOIS 60649

Acknowledgment

We would like to acknowledge the China Conservation and Research Center for the Giant Panda at Wolong Nature Reserve, the leading and largest research facility studying giant pandas in China. The center has been home to about 100 giant pandas.

Researchers at Wolong have made important advances in the study of panda breeding and the care of newborn pandas. One of their ultimate goals is the release of pandas bred at the center into the wild to help ensure the survival of these endangered animals.

The photographs in this book were taken prior to the devastating earthquake of May 2008, centered not far from the Wolong Nature Reserve in southwest China. The earthquake caused much destruction throughout the area, including the structures at the research facilities. Sadly, one giant panda died and another escaped.

When aftershocks caused landslides and threatened more damage, most of the remaining pandas were moved temporarily to other panda shelters in China. The Chinese government has committed funds to rebuild the center as soon as possible so the work with these precious pandas at Wolong can resume.

More information about the China Conservation and Research Center for the Giant Panda can be found at www.pandaclub.net.

Collins is an imprint of HarperCollins Publishers.
Panda Kindergarten

Text copyright © 2009 by Joanne Ryder   Photographs copyright © 2009 by Dr. Katherine Feng/Globio.org/Minden Pictures   Manufactured in China.  All rights reserved. No part of this book may be used or reproduced in any manner whatsoever without written permission except in the case of brief quotations embodied in critical articles and reviews.   For information address HarperCollins Children's Books, a division of HarperCollins Publishers, 1350 Avenue of the Americas, New York, NY 10019.  www.harpercollinschildrens.com

Library of Congress Cataloging-in-Publication Data
Ryder, Joanne.   Panda kindergarten / by Joanne Ryder ; photographs by Dr. Katherine Feng. — 1st ed.
p.   cm.   ISBN 978-0-06-057850-3 (trade bdg.)
1. Giant panda—Anecdotes—Juvenile literature.   I. Title.   QL737.C214R935   2009   599.789—dc22   2008026826   CIP   AC
Designed by Stephanie Bart-Horvath   09 10 11 12 13 SCP 10 9 8 7 6 5 4 3 2 1  ❖   First Edition